Greatest Inventions

Nancy Castaldo

RANDOM HOUSE 🏠 NEW YORK

Published in the United States by Random House Children's Books, a division of Penguin Random House LLC, New York.

Random House and the colophon are registered trademarks of Penguin Random House LLC.

Visit us on the Web! randomhousekids.com

Educators and librarians, for a variety of teaching tools, visit us at RHTeachersLibrarians.com

Library of Congress Cataloging-in-Publication Data is available upon request.

ISBN 978-1-101-93340-4 (trade) — ISBN 978-1-101-93341-1 (lib. bdg.) — ISBN 978-1-101-93342-8 (ebook)

Printed in the United States of America

10 9 8 7 6 5 4 3 2 1

Random House Children's Books supports the First Amendment and celebrates the right to read.

Contents

Note to Readers

What do dragons have to do with real-life science and history?
More than you might think!

For thousands of years, cultures all over the world have told stories about dragons, just as they told fanciful tales about unicorns, fairies, mermaids, ogres, and other mythical creatures. People made up these and other legends for many reasons: to explain the natural world, to give their lives deeper meaning, sometimes even just for fun! Stories passed down from generation to generation began to change over time. In many cases, fact (what's true) and fiction (what's made up) blended together to create a rich legacy of storytelling.

So even though you don't see them flying overhead, dragons are all around us! They are a part of our history and culture, bridging the gap between the past and the present — what's real and what's born of our limitless imaginations. This makes the *DreamWorks Dragons* Dragon Riders ideal candidates to teach us about our world!

Think of the School of Dragons series as your treasure map to a land of fascinating facts about science, history, mythology, culture, innovation, and more! You can read the books cover to cover or skip around to sections that most interest you. There's no right or wrong way when it comes to learning.

And that's not all! When you're done reading the books, you can go online to schoolofdragons.com to play the interactive School of Dragons video games from JumpStart. There's no end to what you can discover. Be sure to check out the inside back cover of this book for a special game code that will allow you access to super-secret adventures!

All ready? Hold on tight, dragon trainers! Here we go . . .

Meet the Characters

Astrid

Hiccup

Snotlout

Fishlegs

Stoick the Vast

Gobber

Ruffnut & Tuffnut

Meet the Dragons

Toothless
Species: Night Fury

Barf & Belch
Species: Hideous Zippleback

Hookfang

Species: Monstrous Nightmare

Meatlug

Species: Gronckle

Stormfly

Species: Deadly Nadder

Weapons

Throughout history, whenever something is difficult, people try to invent ways to make it easier. From the wheel to the smartphone, we've come up with amazing solutions to our everyday problems. Some inventions are discovered by accident, but most are the result of imagination and hard work. Let's look at a few that have made a big impact on history and our lives.

I make the best Viking weapons on Berk!

CROSSBOW

Invented by the Chinese over 2,000 years ago, the **crossbow** changed the way ancient armies battled. The distance an arrow can be shot with a standard bow is limited by the archer's arm length. A crossbow can be shot by anyone able to pull the trigger.

An illustration of crossbow archery from 1555

The crossbow is essentially a bow mounted on a horizontal piece of wood with a trigger that releases the bowstring. The trigger has to be carefully crafted. If it is off by just a tiny bit, it won't work. Though it took longer to load than

A wooden crossbow from Italy

a traditional bow, the crossbow enabled ancient armies to fire many more arrows, darts, or stones than the traditional bow they had been using. Archers could reach targets up to 650 feet away!

Crossbows were used in war until the seventeenth century by many people, including the Chinese, the Greeks, and the Crusaders. Pope Innocent III banned the use of crossbows by Christians against Christians in the Middle Ages, but because crossbows were so effective in warfare, their use eventually became essential. Today, crossbows are mainly used for hunting and target shooting.

CATAPULT

The **catapult** was an important weapon for ancient armies because it could volley objects much farther than a human could throw them. The device was invented around 400 BCE by Dionysius the Elder. He was the ruler of the Greek colony of Syracuse in Sicily and was preparing for a long war with Carthage. Dionysius was looking for a new type of weapon that could be used to shoot arrows or stones at advancing enemies.

A medieval catapult

In Greek, *catapult* means "to throw into." The early catapult could be fired by bracing it against the stomach. These catapults were sometimes called "belly bows." Later designs were larger

11

A medieval catapult at a castle in Tarifa, Spain

and sat upon a stand. This enabled even bigger, more dangerous objects to be hurled at armies or fortresses, including spears, flaming oil, and even the dead bodies of people and animals (the smell of which was then believed to cause disease).

In time, catapults were able to fire weapons with more accuracy. This allowed targets to be hit more easily. Catapults were mainly used to attack city walls or towers.

We Vikings use catapults to attack the enemy.

GUNPOWDER

Gunpowder was invented in China around 850 CE and has been used as an explosive in everything from fireworks to firearms. Alchemists—people who studied the chemical and "magical" properties of different substances—were trying to invent a potion that would grant the drinker eternal life. The potion they created used saltpeter, sulfur, and charcoal. But rather than helping people live longer, it exploded with a bang.

Gunpowder

The early Chinese used the mixture to create fireworks. In addition, the explosive helped them fight their enemy, the Mongols, with flaming arrows that looked like miniature rockets. The powder was used to create land mines and a kind of hand grenade. By the late thirteenth century, gunpowder was used in firearms.

If you upset a Terrible Terror, it lights up the night with its fire.

BODY ARMOR

Body armor is a type of clothing or shield that is used to protect the body from injury. The first armor was made from animal hides to protect wearers from the blows of clubs.

Ancient Greek fighters carried flat, round bronze shields that were layered with animal hides and wax. In medieval Europe, men going into battle wore chain-mail armor made from thousands of tiny metal links. During the fourteenth century, small plates of metal armor were added to the mail to better protect vulnerable areas from weapons like the crossbow.

Ancient Greeks using weapons and shields in the Battle of Mantinea

Early medieval armor

By the mid-fourteenth century, advances in technology—namely the high-velocity crossbow and longbow—necessitated steel-plate armor that covered the body from head to toe. Eventually, this led to the creation of full suits of plate armor in the fifteenth century.

Many types of body armor are still used today, including bomb suits, helmets, shields, and bullet-resistant vests. They are used by military personnel, police, security guards, and hostage rescue teams. As weapons continue to develop, so does protective clothing. Most modern body armor used by the military is made of a strong synthetic fabric called Kevlar, which was invented by chemist Stephanie Kwolek in the 1960s.

A police officer wearing protective clothing

A Dragon Rider needs the right armor.

Transportation

Inventions have opened up our universe. They enable us to travel and explore, to see worlds that are far away, and others that are invisible to the naked eye!

WHEEL

Look at all the things around you that have wheels. There are a lot, right? It may seem like a simple thing to use a round object to move another object along the ground, but surprisingly, the **wheel** was not one

An early stone wheel

of mankind's first inventions. In fact, cloth, rope, and even the flute were invented before the wheel.

Early humans created round objects that could be rolled along the ground, but figuring out how to attach them to a stable platform—such as a wagon or a cart—that moved in a straight line was a difficult task. The wheel-axle combination is the invention that solved the problem.

Picture the wheels on a skateboard. Each pair of wheels is connected by a pole. That pole—or axle—is attached through a hole in the wheels. If the axle is not smooth and round, the wheels won't roll properly. In addition, an axle has to be the correct size so that the wheels can move freely

Modern-day skateboards use wheels and axles

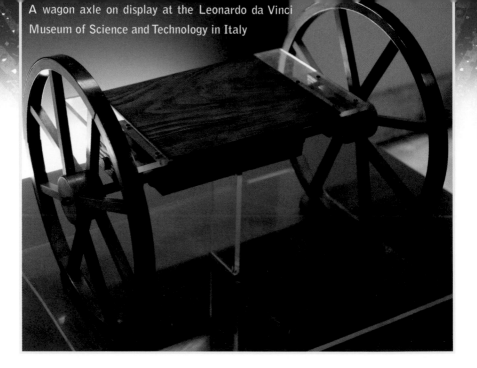

A wagon axle on display at the Leonardo da Vinci Museum of Science and Technology in Italy

without getting stuck. A hole that is too small will make an axle jam.

Experts believe the wheel was invented around 3500 BCE. It became widely used so quickly, however, that they can't be sure exactly *where* it was invented. The oldest-known wheel is believed to be from Mesopotamia (present-day Iraq), but words associated with wheels and wagons come from the region that is modern-day Ukraine, which leads researchers to believe that the wheel was invented by people who lived in that region.

BOAT

Have you ever sailed on a lake or river? **Boats** are used to transport people and goods from one place to another. They can be used for anything from fishing to sailing across the ocean.

Primitive boats, like dugout canoes, were made from hollowed-out logs. Rafts were made from reeds that were bound together. Both were used by people near waterways for thousands of years.

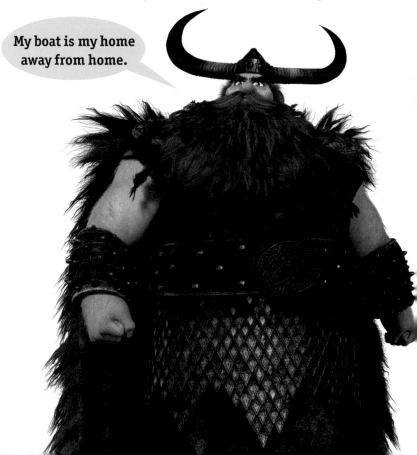

My boat is my home away from home.

Would you want to sail across the ocean on a dugout canoe or a raft? Probably not, as it would be very dangerous! Primitive boats limited the distance people could travel.

The invention of a wooden boat constructed with a **keel** and a **ribbed frame** changed the way boats were made, enabling them to be used on longer journeys. A keel is the piece of a boat that runs along the center of the hull from bow to stern. This kind of boat has ribs—just like we do—that form the structure of the boat. It is believed that the first boats using a keel and a ribbed frame were produced around 4000–3500 BCE in Mesopotamia or Asia. Archaeologists have found that the ancient

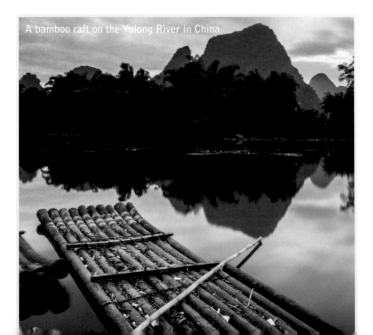
A bamboo raft on the Yulong River in China

Egyptians and Mesopotamians sailed boats built out of cedar wood up and down the Nile River around 3000 BCE. The direction of the river made it easy for Egyptians to sail their boats south with a large sail, but when they wanted to go north, they had to use muscle power to row.

Even though there are many other ways to travel and move goods, we still use ships today to transport things across the globe.

LIGHTHOUSE

Lighthouses are tall buildings that guide ships on waterways. They warn sailors of dangerous coastlines and shallow reefs, and help mark safe harbor entries. The oldest-known lighthouse—the lighthouse of Alexandria—is one of the Seven Wonders of the World.

An illustration of the lighthouse of Alexandria

The ancient Egyptian city of Alexandria had two harbors. One was on the Nile River. The other was on the Mediterranean Sea. Both served the

My dragon will light the way!

city well. Sea trade made the city very wealthy, but there was a huge problem for the busy sailors of Alexandria. Trade ships would leave during the day when it was still light, but sometimes they had to return in the dark or in bad weather. This made it difficult to see the port where they had to dock.

To solve this problem, a tower was built around 280 BCE. It was taller than any other building nearby. At the top of the tower was a great flaming torch. A giant curved mirror reflected the firelight into the dark sky. It was said that sailors could see the light and locate the harbor from 100 miles away. This helped them sail safely into port on a foggy day or dark night.

The Portland Head Light after sunset in Cape Elizabeth, Maine

COMPASS

A **compass** uses a magnetized pointer to show the direction of north. Once you know where north is, you can locate the directions of east, west, and south. Who needs GPS when you have a compass and a map?

Before the invention of the compass, navigation was very difficult. Sailors used the stars and geographical points, like mountains, to point their direction. They would often become lost in bad weather. Ancient Romans found it safe to sail in

An ancient brass compass and sundial

the better weather between June and mid-September, when there was a greater chance for clear skies.

The compass was invented in China somewhere between 200 BCE and 200 CE. The early Chinese compass was made of lodestone—a naturally magnetic mineral—that was carved in a spoon shape and placed on a flat

piece of bronze. The stone spun with the handle of the spoon always facing south. This early compass was called a south-pointer. The first compasses were used by fortune-tellers. They believed the compass could help them find answers to questions. By the eleventh century, the compass was being used by the Chinese for navigation.

Our modern magnetic compass was invented around the fourteenth century in Amalfi, Italy. This north-pointing compass ushered in an era of greater nautical exploration, trade, and discovery. For once, clear skies were not necessary for navigation.

Have you ever gone orienteering or geocaching? These are great ways to test your compass skills and have tons of fun. Search out local orienteering and geocaching events in your area and experience your own treasure hunt.

Magnetic compass

ODOMETER

You've probably seen an **odometer** while riding in a car. This important instrument helps us to measure the distance between one point and another, like a ruler. Before odometers existed, people didn't know exactly how far apart places were. Once a standard measurement—like a mile—was agreed upon, a tool was needed to make those very large measurements.

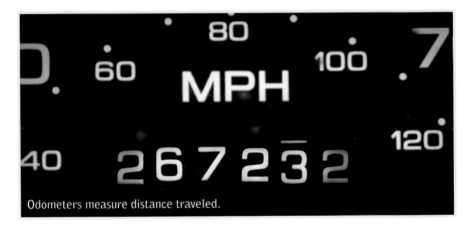

Odometers measure distance traveled.

Roman architect and engineer Vitruvius invented an early odometer around 27 BCE. He mounted a large wheel on a wheelbarrow-like structure. Vitruvius knew the exact circumference

The fastest way between two points is on Barf and Belch.

of, or distance around, the wheel. When the wheel was pushed along the ground, it dropped a pebble into a container every time the wheel went completely around.

Once Vitruvius counted how many pebbles had dropped into the container, he was able to take that number and multiply it by the measurement of the circumference of the wheel. This gave him the distance the odometer had traveled.

Other people improved on this design, including Benjamin Franklin. As postmaster of Philadelphia, Franklin created a simple odometer in 1775 that attached near the wheels of his carriage to measure the distance of his mail route. The odometer measured the circumference of the wheel and the number of revolutions it took to reach one mile. In 1763, he used this odometer to measure the roads between Philadelphia and Boston to calculate the distance he traveled to inspect his post offices.

Fun Fact: You can find out the circumference of a round object yourself by measuring it with a flexible tape measure.

CANAL

Canals are waterways, like rivers, created to allow boats to travel inland or to irrigate crops. The first canals were built for irrigation by the ancient Mesopotamians to control the Euphrates and Tigris Rivers. These canals allowed the Mesopotamians to flood areas that needed water and block off the flow of water when it was too great.

Other canals were also built during ancient times. Chinese engineers are credited with creating many early canals. When Emperor Yang of the

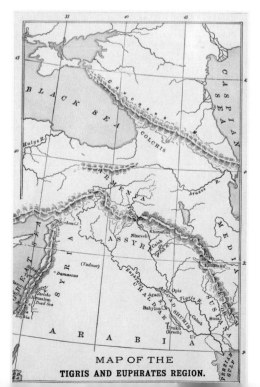

The Tigris and Euphrates river system is located in southwestern Asia.

MAP OF THE
TIGRIS AND EUPHRATES REGION.

Sui dynasty began building the Grand Canal in the seventh century, it was considered a brilliant but nearly impossible idea. The emperor wanted a way to move rice from one area of his kingdom to another to feed his court and his armies. It took an estimated one million workers six years to build

Rivers and oceans are where you can find Thornado and Seashockers.

A modern-day riverboat transports goods on the Yangtze River in China.

the canal. Once created, it allowed barges to travel from the Yangtze River all the way to the Yellow River. By the thirteenth century, the canal had grown and linked the five main rivers in China. It is still in use today, carrying goods, food, soldiers, and ideas across China.

Irrigation means to bring water to land so that farmers can plant crops.

An irrigation system pumps water from the Nile River in Egypt.

Lock

A portrait of Leonardo da Vinci by Cosimo Colombini

Locks are an important invention that enabled canals to be even more useful to transportation. They raise and lower boats between different levels of water on the canal. While canal locks had been used for centuries, it was Leonardo da Vinci who invented the modern canal lock in 1480. Da Vinci's lock was easier to operate and safer for people traveling in boats. This improved lock made it possible for many more canals to be built, allowing people and goods to be transported throughout the world.

RAILROAD

There is nothing like riding the rails and watching out the window as a train chug-chugs down the tracks.

An old steam train

Our modern **railroad** began in 1815, when Colonel John Stevens acquired the first railroad charter in North America. He founded the New Jersey Railroad Company and constructed what he called a steam wagon, the first U.S. steam locomotive, in 1825.

This was just the start of a booming industry. By the 1840s, there were over 2,800 miles of railroad track in the country. By 1850, that number had more than tripled! Trains were here to stay.

When the Civil War ended in 1865, there was 35,000 miles of railroad track in the United States. The country was still very spread out, and the railroad began connecting America's small towns. It was a lot easier to travel by train on smooth rails than over rough roads by horse and wagon. The transcontinental railroad—designed with rails to connect the east coast and west coast of the United States—transformed how Americans traveled.

Train travel has improved a lot since those early days. The invention of automatic train car couplers, air brakes, and new kinds of freight cars launched a new era on the rails. Soon trains were able to run on schedule. By 1916, there were more than 250,000 miles of tracks in the country. Today, an estimated 650,000 people buzz through New York's Pennsylvania Station each day. Amtrak, one of the largest rail carriers in the country, reports that they serve around 31.6 million passengers a year.

CAR

People drive **cars** all over the world to get from place to place. Before cars, horses were the main form of transportation. The horses clippity-clopped over cobblestones and dirt roads, pulling carriages full of people and packages. But horses were far from perfect. Like humans, they required food, water, and rest on long trips.

Then came Henry Ford. While Ford did not invent the car, he developed a way to produce a vehicle that was simple, reliable, and less expensive than other automobiles. In 1903, he began

A Ford Model T car, made in 1925.

We can never make up our minds on where to go.

the Ford Motor Company to produce horseless carriages. He rolled out the first—the Model T—just five years later. There was such a demand for this revolutionary vehicle that the company had to develop a faster way to produce them. In 1913, the world's first moving assembly line for cars was created.

Ford car assembly line in Michigan, circa 1912

AIRPLANE

Since ancient times, people have dreamed of flying. They have strapped wings to their bodies, built machines that flapped their wings like a bird, and lifted off in hot-air balloons. But it wasn't until 1903, near Kitty Hawk, North Carolina, that Orville and Wilbur Wright

Orville and Wilbur W

made the first successful flight of a self-propelled, heavier-than-air aircraft. Today, **airplanes** transport 8 million people every day.

The first commercial airplane flight took place on January 1, 1914, with only one passenger. That's quite different from the 525 passengers who can

My favorite way to fly is on Toothless.

fly on an Airbus A380 today! Not only do planes continue to transport people, but they also move about 55 million tons of cargo each year.

So how do planes fly? The wings are the key. Airplanes have specially designed wings that are shaped so that air moves faster over the top of the wing than under the bottom. This causes

A modern-day commercial aircraft

air pressure on top of the wing to be less than air pressure on the bottom. The difference in this

pressure creates a force on the wing that lifts the plane into the air. At the same time, the plane's engine thrust is greater than the air resistance pulling the plane backward. This moves the plane forward through the air.

You may think that airplane technology has come as far as it can, but every year, there are more improvements in flight. Rockets have left the Earth. Drones may soon deliver our packages. And in 2015, a solar-powered plane took off to complete a flight all the way around the world! What will be next?

A drone

44

Clocks, Watches, and Scientific Instruments

Civilization moved forward by leaps and bounds with the invention of clocks, watches, and other scientific instruments. They connect us, keep us on schedule, and help us explore the world. What would we do without these important inventions?

I'm an inventor, too! I fixed Toothless' tail.

CLOCK

How many times a day do you check the time? Probably more than you realize. **Clocks** help to keep us in sync. Today, we use watches, clocks, and our phones to keep track of time. They keep us from missing important events, like when the school day is over!

Now imagine using only the sun to tell time. Sure, you'd know when it was morning or night, but would you know when to turn on your favorite TV show? The sundial was the first device invented to measure time. As its name implies, it used the path of the sun to measure the passage of hours.

When the sun comes up, we'd rather be sleeping!

A modern-day sundial

It is not known who invented the sundial, but it was used by many ancient civilizations, including the Egyptians, Greeks, and Romans. The device was around for centuries (and is still in use today), but it is flawed. Sundials can only be used when the sun is out, and they are unable to maintain a constant division of time, like hours, minutes, and seconds. You can't, for example, use a sundial to time a three-minute egg!

Ancient Egyptians also used a water clock that used two containers of water at different heights. Hours were measured by the flow of the water from the higher container into

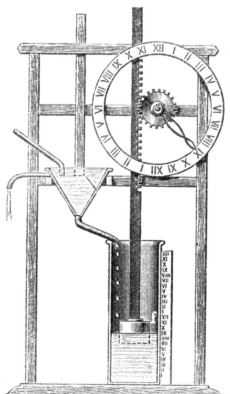
A water clock

the lower container. Lines measured the water levels. The earliest known water clock was found in the tomb of the Egyptian pharaoh Amenhotep I, who lived during the sixteenth century BCE.

Ancient Greeks used a water clock that they called a clepsydra, or "water thief." The Greeks used the clocks to time the speeches of famous orators and philosophers, like Aristotle. But like the sundial, the water clock was not perfect. The length of days and nights varied with the seasons, and it was difficult to keep the pressure of the water flow constant.

Time flies when you're a Dragon Rider.

TELESCOPE

A **telescope** lets us see things that are very far away—like stars in the sky, or a distant port from the bow of a ship—and makes them seem like they are much closer.

Hans Lippershey is credited with inventing the first telescope in 1608. He was an eyeglass maker in the Netherlands and made lenses. He put a convex lens (one that curves out) and a concave

A modern-day telescope

Convex and concave lenses

lens (one that curves in) together and discovered that he could see things that were far away as if they were up close. His device was able to magnify things three times.

In 1609, the Italian astronomer Galileo Galilei built his own telescope. He made the telescope famous. Galileo's devices were able to magnify things twenty times. Among his many famous telescopic discoveries was finding the four moons circling around the planet Jupiter. These are now known as the Galilean moons.

Galileo demonstrating his telescope

WRISTWATCH

The *New York Times* wrote about the curious trend of people in Europe wearing bracelets with clocks on them in 1916. It was odd behavior, and most people thought it was just a new fashion trend. But **wristwatches** were more than that—they told people what time it was quicker than pulling a watch out of their pocket.

A modern wristwatch

Before the twentieth century, only women wore watches. But during World War I, soldiers in Europe began wearing watches with unbreakable glass. They also used radium to make the numbers glow in the dark. These newfangled wrist clocks were very valuable in the trenches.

Not long after, the world entered into another war. Wristwatches used by the U.S. military now had a second hand, and watches could be

The inner workings of an old watch

synchronized to the exact second. This helped coordinate the movements of Allied troops as they stormed the beaches of Normandy, France, to fight the Germans on D-Day during World War II. The small invention of a timepiece on the wrist became crucial to the success of the war.

The Allied forces stormed the beaches Normandy, France, on June 6, 1944.

SMARTWATCH

The Dick Tracy comic strip features a police detective who often uses technology to solve crimes. Beginning in 1946, Tracy first wore a very special two-way wrist radio that he could talk into. At the time, there was nothing like it in real life. In 1964, Tracy's innovative wrist radio was upgraded to feature a wrist TV—an equally unheard-of idea! In the 1990 *Dick Tracy* movie, the detective can still be seen communicating on his high-tech wristwatch—one that resembles a present-day **smartwatch.**

A smartwatch is basically a wearable computer and does more than just tell time. Since around 2000, different kinds of smartwatches have been available. In 2015, Apple unveiled their Apple Watch. Not only could wearers listen to music and check their email—they could also talk on the phone!

Apple Watch

Communication

Inventions can bring people together. They let us know what is happening across town—and on the other side of the planet!

Computers can help us to connect with loved ones.

Printing Press

The first **printing press with movable type** was made by a German goldsmith named Johannes Gutenberg around 1440 CE. Before it was invented, books had to be copied by hand or printed using carved wooden blocks that were inked and pressed onto paper. Books were so time-consuming to produce and so costly, few people could afford them.

Gutenberg's movable metal type could be quickly changed and featured both upper- and lowercase letters, numbers, and punctuation marks. Printing books was now easier and less expensive. For the first time, average citizens were able to own books. This made it easier for people to learn to read and to share knowledge.

Meatlug and I have our own way of communicating.

BRAILLE

Before the invention of **Braille** in 1824, people who were sight-impaired had to trace their finger along raised letters in specially made books. Sometimes a single sentence filled a page, and it was very difficult to distinguish between the letters. Reading a book was a slow and difficult task for the sight-impaired. If it wasn't for Louis Braille, it might still be.

Young Louis injured his eye with a sharp tool in his father's leather shop when he was three years old. He developed an infection that spread to his

A statue of Louis Braille as a young boy

While dive-bombing his enemies, Toothless can camouflage himself and blend in within the dark night sky.

other eye and eventually caused him to become completely blind.

Louis learned about a "night writing" system that was developed for the military to communicate in the dark. The system did not prove to be useful, but it did inspire fifteen-year-old Louis to improve upon it and to invent a series of characters made up of raised dots.

Louis assigned to each letter a special arrangement of one to six dots in rows. It allowed for all letters of the alphabet, numbers, and punctuation. The dots could be read as letters and words and became known as Braille. Braille could be written with a tool called a Braillewriter. A Braillewriter was similar to a typewriter. The new system made reading faster and easier.

Although Braille became very popular, it wasn't until Louise Braille died that the National Institute for Blind Youth in Paris, where he was a student and later worked, officially adopted it for their students.

By 1916, Braille had been adopted in almost every language and is now the most common way for blind people to read throughout the world.

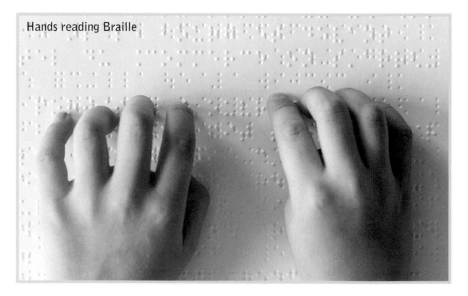

Hands reading Braille

TELEGRAPH

Samuel Morse with the telegraph

Samuel Morse created the first working **telegraph** in the 1830s and 1840s. This revolutionary machine transmitted electrical signals over a wire in a series of dots and dashes that corresponded to the letters of the alphabet. The first telegraph message was sent by Morse in 1844 from Washington, D.C., to Baltimore. Morse's invention enabled people to send messages across many miles throughout the United States but not to Europe.

Cyrus West Field developed the idea for an **under-ocean cable** to connect the United States to

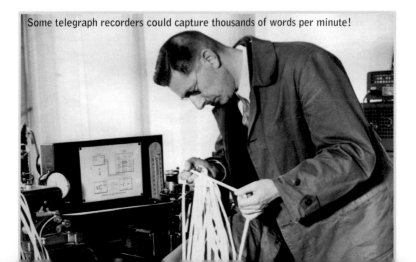

Some telegraph recorders could capture thousands of words per minute!

Europe. By 1858, after four attempts and with the help of naval ships from America and Britain, the first transatlantic cable was laid across the bottom of the Atlantic Ocean from America to Britain.

One of the first telegrams was sent from Queen Victoria to James Buchanan, president of the United States, on August 16, 1858. It began: "The Queen desires to congratulate the President upon the successful completion of this great international work."

The message took sixteen hours to send by Morse code. This may seem like a lot of time, but to people who were used to sending letters to Europe via ship, the speed was amazing.

hip taking aboard cable to connect
United States with Europe

Hookfang and I always talk it out!

TELEPHONE

Telephones allow us to talk to people all over the world. But before the invention of the telephone in 1876, people had to rely on writing letters to get their message across. It could take days or even months for a letter to be received. Mail was delivered on horseback by the riders of the Pony Express or by railroad. Either way, it had to be carried over a distance, which took time.

Alexander Graham Bell makes a call to Thomas Watson.

Alexander Graham Bell was an American inventor who wanted to solve that problem. While trying to invent a device to carry many messages on a single wire, Bell heard the sound of a plucked spring along sixty feet of wire. This led him to experiment with sending a human voice over a wire.

He succeeded! Bell made the very first phone call on March 10, 1876. He called his assistant, Thomas A. Watson, who was in the next room. He said, "Mr. Watson—come here—I want to see you." What would *you* have said?

PHOTOGRAPH

It is estimated that more than 880 billion **photographs** are taken each year. All these images connect us with people and events and help preserve our history.

Early cameras used a pinhole for a lens and projected the reverse image of an object onto a viewing surface. Called a camera obscura, the principle behind the device probably dates back to ancient Greece. But images from a camera obscura needed to be traced onto paper. There was no way to preserve them like we can with photographs today.

The use of photographic film was pioneered by George Eastman. He also developed cameras that were smaller and less expensive than

An advertisement for the Kodak camera from 1890

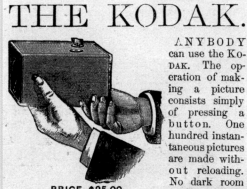

THE KODAK.

ANYBODY can use the Ko-DAK. The operation of making a picture consists simply of pressing a button. One hundred instantaneous pictures are made without reloading. No dark room or chemicals are

PRICE, $25.00.

necessary. A division of labor is offered, whereby all the work of finishing the pictures is done at the factory, where the camera can be sent to be reloaded. The operator need not learn anything about photography. He can "*press the button*"—*we do the rest*.

Send for copy of KODAK Primer, with sample photograph.

The Eastman Dry Plate and Film Co.,
ROCHESTER, N. Y.

others. In 1886, Eastman introduced the first Kodak camera. Two years later, the first rolls of flexible film went on sale. This made photography available to many more people. It seems unlikely that Eastman could have dreamed how photography would take off. Today, we take as many photos every two minutes as were taken in the entire 1800s—only now we use film cameras, digital cameras, and even cameras on our phones.

We've come a long way since those early cameras and film. This is a good example of how inventions keep changing. People are always inventing new ways to make things better.

Two kids use a selfie stick to capture a pho

RADIO

Radio enabled us to instantly hear about things happening on the other side of the neighborhood or on the other side of the planet. Nowadays, hundreds of millions of people listen to the radio each week.

There is a debate over who discovered radio. Serbian-American scientist Nikola Tesla and Italian physicist Guglielmo Marconi each played an important part in its invention.

In 1891, Tesla invented a coil (named the Tesla coil) that enabled people to send and receive messages through telegraphy. This coil was needed for a radio to work. Unfortunately, as Tesla was finally ready to send his first radio signal, a fire destroyed his laboratory.

At the same time,

Marconi was conducting experiments in wireless telegraphy. In 1896, he sent and received radio signals from about four miles away. Both Tesla and Marconi filed patents for their radio inventions, claiming ownership. In 1900, the U.S. Patent Office granted Tesla patents for the Tesla coil. That same year, Marconi filed a patent for tuned telegraphy, another important part of the radio. Marconi's patent was first rejected because it relied on Tesla's work, but four years later, the Patent Office reversed its decision. Marconi received his patent and was credited with inventing the radio.

Marconi's Wireless Telegraph Company was

Radios have been manufactured in all different shapes and sizes.

thriving in Britain, and he gained financial support from Thomas Edison and investor Andrew Carnegie. Stocks soared. In 1909, Marconi achieved fame for the first transmission of radio signals across the Atlantic Ocean. That year he also received the Nobel Prize for Physics for his work on the radio. This infuriated Tesla, and he took Marconi to court over patent infringement. In 1943 (two years after Tesla's death), the Supreme Court ruled that Marconi's patents were invalid and that Tesla was the inventor of the radio.

TELEVISION

Turn on the **television,** and you can see a rocket launch into space, an earthquake's devastation on the other side of the world, or an animated cartoon that makes you giggle. Television connects, entertains, and informs us about our world. It brings picture and sound into our homes. Before the TV existed, people relied on radios, newspapers, and newsreels at the movies to get information. TV changed all that. It reaches millions of people as things happen. It has brought world events into our living rooms.

Sometimes television gives us a window on history, like when the moon landing was broadcast on July 20, 1969. And when Richard Nixon sweated under the hot lights during the 1960 presidential election debate, while young, attractive John F. Kennedy remained cool and collected, voters were swayed. Television changed history!

Richard Nixon, left, and John F. Kennedy, right, in a televised 1960 presidential debate

Where radio moves sound waves through the air, television moves images and sounds over wires or through the air using electrical impulses.

Many people contributed to the invention of television as we know it today. Philo Taylor Farnsworth is one of the inventors who contributed to the development of the modern television. When he was twenty-one, Farnsworth made his first successful electronic television transmission. It's amazing to think that Farnsworth grew up without electricity in his home until he was fourteen.

Considering the number of channels available on TV today, it's hard to believe that at one time there were only three—ABC, CBS, and NBC! In the beginning, television was only available in black-and-white. The United States was the first country to introduce color television in 1950, on CBS. By the late 1970s, most countries had color television. Today, there are many ways to receive television into our homes, including cable television and satellite. We can even watch TV on our phones!

Ballpoint Pen

Before the invention of the **ballpoint pen,** people used fountain pens that needed to be filled with ink from a bottle. But fountain pens were messy! The ink took a long time to dry on the paper and often smudged. The tip of the pen would sometimes scratch and tear through paper. Have you ever had a pen leak or smudge? Then you know how frustrating this can be!

Fountain pen with a bottle of ink

The first person who developed and successfully sold a ballpoint pen with a pressurized ink cartridge was Laszlo Biro in 1938. His pen didn't need to be dipped into an inkwell as he wrote. As a journalist and artist, he saw how newspaper ink dried quickly without smudges. But newspaper ink was thick and couldn't be used in a fountain pen. Biro had the idea to create a tiny ball at the tip of his pen that was able to move along a piece of paper while picking up ink from the cartridge inside. His brother Gyorgy, a chemist, helped him to create an ink that would work with his new pen.

Biro's pen became very popular. The first bulk order of 30,000 pens was placed by the British Royal Air Force. In 1945, American businessman Milton Reynolds copied Biro's design and began selling pens at Gimbels department store in New York City. Within days, they had sold thousands. The ballpoint pen device revolutionized how we communicate with each other through writing, making it fast and easy to spread ideas. In fact, you can still find pens manufactured by Bic that say "Biro" on them today—in recognition of the pen's first designers.

A Biro by Bic pen

Biro by **BIC** MED.

COMPUTER

Computers have changed the way we find out about the world and how we communicate with others. It's hard to believe that as recently as 1955 there were only 250 computers on the entire planet. The computers that did exist then were so big they took up entire rooms! The invention

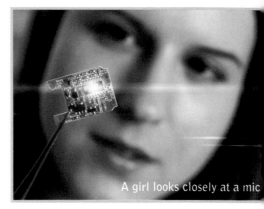

A girl looks closely at a mic

of the **microchip,** a tiny electronic circuit, led the way for much smaller computers, like tablets and personal computers.

A family shopping together online

Today, we can even work on our computers outside!

The invention of the personal desktop computer changed the way people communicated and did business, and made computers available to anyone. The first personal computers were sold in the 1970s as kits. People who purchased the kit put the computers together themselves. Monitors, keyboards, and disk drives were not included. Since then, the personal computer has changed and advanced. Inventions and improvements have now brought us devices so small that we can carry them in our pocket. Just as the printing press did, the personal computer changed the way we communicate. Since the 1970s, there have been over a billion computers sold in the world!

VIDEO GAME

The invention of **video games** goes hand in hand with the invention of the computer. Physicist Willy Higinbotham is credited with creating a table-tennis game on a machine called an oscilloscope in Upton, New York, in 1958. In 1966, inventor Ralph Baer conceived the idea for a video game that could be played on a television. A year later, he built a prototype, and in 1968, he received

The Magnavox Odyssey was the first video game console.

Video games can be a lot of fun!

a patent for his invention. In 1972, Magnavox released the Odyssey based on Baer's invention. It was the first home-based video game system. In 1975, Atari introduced *Pong,* a competitor to the Odyssey's table-tennis game, and it became an instant holiday success.

In the following years, video games would find their way from televisions to computers to our smartphones. There is even a National Video Game Museum being built in Texas.

Conclusion

Inventions have opened up the world to us and have made our lives very different from our ancestors'. Who knows what we'll discover next? Pill-sized cameras you swallow to diagnose disease? Invisibility cloaks that make objects seem to disappear? Planes that fold into cars? (In fact, all these things are inventions that really DO exist!)

With a little imagination and a lot of hard work, maybe *you'll* be the person to create the next breakthrough!

Now we know all about inventions. What adventures will we go on next?